Leaning
ON PRAYER

Leaning
ON PRAYER

BY
JERRI A. HARWELL

spring creek
BOOK COMPANY
Provo, Utah

ISBN: 1-932898-26-3
e. 1

Published by:
Spring Creek Book Company
P.O. Box 50355
Provo, Utah 84605-0355

Cover design © Spring Creek Book Company
Cover design by Nicole Cunningham
Cover model: Rene Harwell

Printed in the United States of America
10 9 8 7 6 5 4 3 2 1
Printed on acid-free paper

Library of Congress Control Number: 2004098415

Dedication

I dedicate my first published book to my father,
the late Russell E. Hale, R.Ph. (1916–1990).

When I told him I wanted to be a writer, instead of
going to medical school, he said, with a tear in his eye,
"But baby, your handwriting isn't that damn good."

Acknowledgments

Thank you to Don, Bronson, Richard, Morgan, and Rene for your patience and understanding while I wrote this book. Hey Webe, (short for "We Be a Family With a Dawg") our Shih Tzu – Thanks for sitting at my feet and keeping them warm while I wrote.

A special, thank you to Susan Frampton, with whom I've had many late night chat sessions about prayer. You were the first to hear many of the experiences related in this book and to encourage me to write them down.

To President Darius A. Gray, thanks for the pep talks. Lunch is on me.

To my editors, Cara O'Sullivan, Betsy VanDenBerghe, and Ellen Henneman, thank you for your hours and hours of meticulous editing and proofreading.

To Richard and Marsha Stamps—who embraced me when I joined the Church in the Pontiac Ward in Michigan so many years ago. I will cherish our friendship forever.

Finally, to Elders Russell Rubert and Mark Merrill—the first "Mormon Missionaries" to teach me about the existence of God and how to pray to Him. Thank you for your infinite patience in teaching me how to pray.

Preface

Over the years, as I have taught lessons and given talks in church or at firesides, the stories that have been received well are my experiences with prayer. For years people have been encouraging me to write a book, especially about prayer and how to recognize answers.

My references are few because I have really learned how to pray by praying. I have, however, found two books extremely useful: *Prayer* published by Deseret Book and *Do Your Prayers Bounce Off the Ceiling?* By Grant S. Worth.

Both books are out of print, but you might be able to find copies in used bookstores, especially in and around Utah. *Prayer* is a compilation of talks and writings by several General Authorities on every aspect of prayer. You will probably find most, if not all, of these talks on the Internet.

If I may use an analogy, just like you do not learn to drive a car by reading the owner's manual or drivers' education books, you cannot learn to pray by reading books. You can learn about prayer by reading, but reading is not praying.

After reading *Prayer*, I typed a copy of a paragraph that I felt would help me to focus my prayers. For weeks and months I read the following passage before every prayer. I carried this typed sheet tucked inside my scripture covers, and it still sits in my scriptures to this day. The passage is from Bishop H. Burke Peterson's "Adversity and Prayer," (pp. 108–9). It reads: "As you feel the need to confide in the Lord or to improve the quality of your visits with him—to pray, if you please—may I suggest a process to follow: go where you can be alone, where you can think, where you can kneel, where you can speak out loud to him. The bedroom, the bathroom, or a closet will do. Now, picture him in your mind's eye. Think to whom you are speaking. Control your thoughts—don't let them wander. Address him as your Father and your friend. Now tell him things you really feel to tell him—not trite phrases that have little meaning, but a sincere, heartfelt conversation with him. Confide in him. Ask him for forgiveness. Plead with him. Enjoy him. Thank him. Express your love to him. Then listen for his answers. Listening is an essential part of praying. Answers from the Lord come quietly, ever so quietly. In fact, few hear his answers audibly with their ears. We must be listening carefully or we will never recognize them. Most answers from the Lord are felt in our hearts as a warm, comfortable expression, or they may come as thoughts to our minds. They come to those who are prepared and who are patient." Peterson concludes, "For your own good [you] must take the first step, and this step is prayer."

Jerri A. Harwell
November 2004

CHAPTER ONE

Taking the First Step and Yearning to Pray

"I would exhort you that ye would ask God, the Eternal Father, in the name of Christ, if these things are not true; and if ye shall ask with a sincere heart, with real intent, having faith in Christ, he will manifest the truth of it unto you by the power of the Holy Ghost."

—MORONI 10:4

My first memories of praying were made in Winona, West Virginia, while visiting my dad's sister, Aunt Newassa. Every night she would have me kneel by the side of my bed and pray. It was the simplest prayer and one I could make as long or as short as I wanted.

If I wanted a long prayer, I would ask God to bless every member of my family including the dogs (ours and my aunt's). "Dear God, bless Momma, bless Daddy, bless

LaClaire, bless Jacob, bless Odessa, bless Uncle Happy, bless Aunt Newassa " and on and on until I had mentioned everyone or until I was too tired to keep going.

If I wanted a short prayer, I would put everyone in a collective group except for the dogs because I figured the people could really pray for themselves, but the dogs couldn't. "Dear God, bless my family and Aunt Newassa (she was kneeling next to me, so I thought it was polite to single her out) and all my aunts and uncles, and the dogs in my life—Prince, Rusty, Sparkle . . ."

Those prayers seemed to satisfy my aunt, and it seemed special because I prayed only when I visited her. Sometimes I'd add the following prayer: "Now I lay me down to sleep. I pray the Lord my soul to keep. If I should die before I wake, I pray the Lord my soul to take." But I really only did that so my aunt would be impressed that I had memorized something.

That was the extent of my praying until I was an adult. In 1976, I was seventeen and back then I was a huge fan of the Osmonds. I watched their appearances on TV every chance I got. One evening I sat down to watch a show titled "The Family and Other Living Things," which The Church of Jesus Christ of Latter-day Saints (LDS Church) produced. I wanted to see it because, according to *TV Guide*, the Osmonds were scheduled to appear. It took so long for the Osmonds to appear that I ended up watching the entire show. As I recall, a 1-800 number popped up for viewers to call and get a free brochure about the principles of the show I had just watched. Being a freshman at Oakland University in Rochester, Michigan, and living in a campus dormitory, I thought this would be a great way to get some mail. I called and sent for the brochure. When it arrived, I stuck it in a drawer without reading it. Several weeks later while cleaning out the drawer, I came across the brochure. I thumbed through it and found a prepaid postage card that I could send in and get more information about the Latter-day Saint Church. I thought, "Good, I can get some more mail." Not too long afterward, two *male* missionaries called me.

They wanted to schedule an appointment to talk with me about the Church. I set an appointment for the next day, Saturday. I hung up the phone and went on campus to see a student production. All evening I kept trying to talk myself out of the appointment I had scheduled for the next day. Why should I waste my time listening to missionaries? I didn't go to church because I didn't even believe there was a God. Oh well, I decided, I'll just listen to them for a few minutes and then tell them I have something else to do. That will get rid of them.

The next morning, in preparation for the Mormon missionaries, I cleaned my room up and moved all the alcohol bottles out of sight. I didn't drink at the time, but I did collect the large bottles the alcohol came in. I threw something over the bottles even though they were in my closet; I didn't want to take any chances with them thinking I had an alcohol problem. I couldn't do anything about the marijuana plant sitting on the windowsill; it belonged to my roommate. I knew the Osmonds didn't smoke or drink because of their religious beliefs, so I didn't want to offend these guys coming over. (Several years later, Russell Rubert, one of the missionaries who came, told me he'd recognized the marijuana plant in the windowsill. He and his companion, Mark Merrill, just never questioned me about it.)

The next day, the missionaries arrived as scheduled. When they saw me, Elder Rubert's eyebrows went up. He asked if I really wanted "to be taught about the Church," because he didn't want to do anything he wasn't supposed to do. I thought that was an odd question, but I said yes and let them in. I told them I had about an hour and then I had something to do.

They began with a story about Joseph Smith and how he saw God the Father and Jesus Christ. It was so new to me. It was actually interesting. Before long, the missionaries said they had to go because their time was up, but they asked if I had any questions. I looked at the clock and thought to myself that I really wanted them to stay, but I had already lied and told them I had something else to do. Still, I asked several questions about why the Osmonds did things like turning down drinks from dignitaries and why they weren't into drugs. The missionaries explained a little about the Word of Wisdom but not much stuck with me. I was back on the idea of a boy seeing God the Father and Jesus Christ. The missionaries really seemed to believe what they were saying.

Finally they got around to praying, and I let them pray all they wanted. I had no interest in talking to myself in front of people. We scheduled another appointment, and they were off.

I looked through the Book of Mormon they left, but I really didn't read it. They had also left a card, which outlined the four basic steps of prayer. I don't remember when I offered my first prayer as outlined on that card, but I do recall my words and my attitude during that prayer.

I said, "Heavenly Father, if you are really there like these missionaries say you are, will you answer this prayer and let me know? I really don't believe in a God, but if there is one and you're it, maybe you could let me know who you are and what you are. These missionaries really seem to believe you exist, so I just thought I'd ask for myself in case you do exist. In the name of Jesus Christ. Amen."

I paused and listened. What did I hear? Silence. A whole lot of silence. I didn't get anything right then and thought to myself, "Um, just what I thought," and I went to sleep.

Despite my lack of progress in hearing an answer to my initial prayers, I continued to "take the lessons" with the missionaries. I challenged them with question after question, and they always had an answer—even if that answer was a good old-fashioned "I don't know."

I also continued to pray, in faith, hoping some Being was there to answer. One night I found out for myself that He existed. I was saying my usual prayer, praying to know if God existed, but I had added another question that stemmed from a sincere desire to know: was what I was being taught by the Mormon missionaries true? I prayed with a sincere heart. I prayed with all the faith I could muster that my prayer would be answered by someone. I prayed and waited for an answer. Then it came.

A strong, warm burning in my bosom confirmed every prayer I had uttered in the last few weeks. I knew what it meant. I knew who it was from. I knew.

Forgetting about all that formal kneel-down-when-you-pray stuff, I stood up, sat on the bed, and asked, "Now what?" After that prayer, all the missionary lessons fell into place. I understood them, believed them, and knew what a huge commitment it would be to live them. Because I didn't want to commit to "living the gospel" at such an early age, I did not feel compelled to get baptized right away. Elder Rubert and Elder Merrill moved on. Transferred is a term I came to know well. Several sets of missionaries came and went. Some would challenge me to commit to baptism, but I wouldn't go for it. I figured I could keep living life as I was and "get religious" when I was older and ready to settle down.

God had a different plan and a different time line. I guess He had to speed things up for me. During the summer of 1977, I stayed in a single dorm room while I attended summer classes. It was during this time that I started having a series of disturbing dreams. One night I dreamed I was walking toward Satan, the devil, and he was motioning for me to follow him. Off to the right I saw a man in a white robe. I think it could have been Christ, but I'm not sure. The man held out His hand and said, "Take my hand and he [Satan] can never hurt you." I took a few steps toward Him and took His hand. To this day, I have never let go of that hand.

Just a few weeks before I was baptized, I had another dream that prompted me to stop delaying my baptism. In the dream I walked up to a lunch counter and sat down. I looked up and saw someone, or just the face of someone, who seemed to float down to talk to me. I had the feeling it was my oldest sister, Vicki, who died in 1949 when she was less than two weeks old. Obviously, I had never seen her in this world, but I had been asking my mother about her. Vicki said it was a shame people didn't find out about the Mormon Church until it was too late. I agreed and said, "Yes, it is." She then called me by name and told me not to let it happen to me. I told her I wouldn't, and that was the end of the dream.

I woke up scared. I thought I ought to get baptized as soon as possible. I didn't know who the missionaries in the area were—it was hard to keep up with so many who taught me. While walking across campus one day, I saw Professor Richard Stamps, who was a member of the Church and often came with the missionaries to teach me. I recognized him because of the distinctive hats he always wore. I asked him if he knew how I could get in touch with the missionaries. He said he did and that he would have them call me.

The missionaries came over on a Wednesday and asked me to be baptized the next Saturday. The dream came to mind, and I instantly accepted. I still had some doubts because of my parents and my own fear of what was I getting myself into. The night before my scheduled baptism, I called the missionaries to back out. Being dutiful missionaries, they did not allow me to back out. They reminded me not only of the covenant I was about to make but also that they had made a covenant with God to have me baptized the next day.

I was baptized on Saturday, September 17, 1977,

by Neil Ray Keith and confirmed by Richard Brown
Stamps. My parents, Russell and Julia Hale, attended, as
did my college roommate, Pat Golick, a non-practicing
Catholic. During one of the talks, Richard Anderson, a
member of the Pontiac Michigan Ward and counselor in
the bishopric, bore his testimony and said that he knew I
was doing the right thing. I thought to myself, "I'm glad
you know it's right, because I sure don't." I was still scared
of the commitment.

In the months after my baptism, I recorded these
events in my journal. One entry reads: "I have since [my
baptism] had spiritual experiences while praying and these
I feel are personal and can be experienced by anyone
who prays believing and in faith." I'd like to share the
principles of prayer and these spiritual experiences, that I
have leaned on, with you so you too can use these as tools
to communicate effectively with Heavenly Father.

CHAPTER TWO

Learning to Pray

"Search diligently, pray always, and be believing."
—DOCTRINE AND COVENANTS 90:24

After I joined the Church, I immersed myself in doctrinal study, scriptural study, and sometimes my college studies. I was a sophomore without a major. I was in college because my parents wanted me to go, but I didn't know what I wanted to do with my life. I had always said I wanted to go to medical school, but deep down I knew that was really only to please my father and live the life he couldn't live.

Soon after joining the Church, Bishop Foley called me to be the Young Adult Representative and be responsible for organizing activities for the young single adults in the ward. I didn't think I knew enough for such a calling. Being so new in the Church, I wanted to learn and know everything in the first few months. I had to learn to pace myself to learn "line upon line, precept upon precept."

Some days I spent more time reading and studying the scriptures than I spent studying for my classes. Because I spent so much time studying the scriptures and gospel principles, I came to lean on or rely on the Lord to confirm the conclusions I reached during my personal studies. For example, once I was studying a subject by reviewing several scriptures. After deciding I understood the gospel principle, I knelt down and asked Heavenly Father if I understood it correctly. He said, "No, you have not taken into consideration the scripture in . . ."

Amazed at such a clear answer, I got up, turned to the scripture, and realized I had missed a vital point. I reread the passage and some of the others I had studied, and then prayed again. "Heavenly Father, a few minutes ago, I misunderstood this principle, but now having taken into consideration the scripture you brought to my mind I now understand this principle to mean . . ."

"That is correct," was His reply. Wow. The Lord said in D&C 9:7–9 to study a question out in your own mind, reach a conclusion, and then ask Him if it be right. I quickly learned I could take that scripture literally.

This lesson became especially useful when the desire to go on a mission entered my head. One of the young adults in the ward, Neil Keith, had recently returned from serving a mission, and others talked of going. Soon,

I began talking about going on a mission also. I let some of the members know I wanted to serve a mission, and I was met with some resistance. Then I told the second counselor in the bishopric, Richard Anderson, of my desire to serve a mission, and he said he would check to see if I could and get back to me.

When Brother Anderson got back to me, he told me I couldn't serve as a full-time missionary, but I could serve as a local or stake missionary. The problem—I was Black! It seemed the gospel could not be taught to Blacks unless they asked for it. That explained the odd question that Elder Rubert had asked when he first came to my dorm that Saturday. When he had seen that I was Black, he hesitated to teach me unless I asked for the discussions.

While taking the discussions, my parents had told me that Blacks couldn't join the Mormon Church nor could they hold the (Mormon) priesthood. I had asked the missionaries about this, and they were straightforward with me. They had said, "Of course Blacks can be members. But no, Blacks cannot hold the priesthood but someday they will." I had readily accepted their answer because I felt good about it. Being a woman, I couldn't hold the priesthood anyway, so I didn't think too much about it—*until* I was told I couldn't do something such as going on a full-time mission. I was irate. I associated this exclusion with prejudice, and I no longer wanted to be part of the

Church. Still, I had a calling, and because I didn't want anyone else involved in my going inactive, I knew I had to make this issue a matter of earnest and sincere prayer.

For several days afterwards I did not pray, because I could not bring myself to pray to a God who established a Church that excluded Blacks from the priesthood and from serving missions. I didn't want the priesthood. I wanted only to serve a mission. Brother Andersen questioned whom would I teach? I responded that I would teach Whites and anyone else who wanted to hear the gospel. My mother was American Indian, and she asked why I was being excluded if Mormons thought so highly of American Indians. "Why don't they let that part of you go in the temple?" she asked. No one could provide me or my mother with a satisfactory answer.

That week I wrote in my journal: "I seem to hurt all over. Why isn't it time for Blacks to hear about the gospel? How can Heavenly Father be a just God, and not give Blacks a chance to hear the gospel? Why must they first approach the church? Why was I born with Negroid blood? Why me? God, why me?"

Coincidently, I was reading a book titled *Prayer*, which was a compilation of talks and writings by General Authorities on every aspect of prayer. In the same journal entry, I wrote, "I've been reading a book called Prayer. It's very edifying. Now I have a fuller knowledge of prayer.

I shall utilize this knowledge of prayer. I shall utilize this knowledge from now on."

Finally, after resolving not to pray, I found myself on my knees in prayer. I could no longer lean on my own understanding, I needed to understand from the Lord Himself. I was sobbing and pouring my heart out to God. I called on every ounce of knowledge about prayer I had gleaned from the above book and believed with one hundred percent faith that God would hear and answer my prayer. My faith was rewarded. As I ended my prayer asking Heavenly Father why Blacks could not receive the priesthood, I felt a burning and heard the Lord say, "*I* have never given a reason." What? I thought. I had researched and read so much on the priesthood restriction that surely the truth, the reason was in there somewhere. Again the Lord repeated his answer and said, "*I* have never given a reason." I took him at His word. All that I had been reading over the past several months were the opinions of men. The Lord Himself had never given a reason. I set aside all the stuff about curses, indecision, and fence sitters in the premortal life, and Bruce R. McConkie's doctrine. I had heard from the Lord Himself and from that point forward, I did not doubt Him, His answer, or my decision to join the LDS Church.

The next Sunday, I went back to Church and apologized to Brother Anderson for how I had reacted when he told me I couldn't serve a full-time mission. I knew better than to curse in the Lord's house, but I had come pretty darn close. Brother Anderson accepted my apology and told me he loved me and admired my faith.

Still as one last ditch effort, I asked him how anyone knew I was of the lineage whereby I could not serve a mission. He said that perhaps receiving my patriarchal blessing would answer that for me. So after an interview with Bishop Foley, I was off to see our stake patriarch, Samuel S. Skousen. I went fasting and hoping to learn what the Lord had in store for me.

Once I arrived and we chatted a bit, the patriarch laid his hands on my head and proceeded with the blessing. Nothing stood out until the last line, when he advised me, "to be very dedicated to [my] educational pursuits at this time." I almost fell off the chair. I had not told the patriarch that I was considering dropping out of school for a while. After hearing that line, I did stay in school and graduated about eighteen months later. A major struggle for me, while in school, was what to major in. I had no idea what I wanted to do. Sometime later, when I prayed and asked Heavenly Father what I should major in, He said, "I don't care what you major in; I just want you to have a degree."

After the blessing, the patriarch walked me to the door and said, "I hoped that answered some questions for you." I said, "Yes, but I was hoping you would declare my lineage." He gasped and said, "I didn't do that, did I? Wait, come back in. I'll have to do an addendum."

I returned to his office and sat in his chair. A few years later, I learned how unusual it is not to have one's lineage declared in a patriarchal blessing. Now on my blessing I have an addendum given the same night as my blessing. While my blessing does not say which "tribe of Israel" I am from, it does say I am "of the loins of Ham" and I "have the blood of Israel" in me also.

Also of significance is that two to three years later, another patriarch who lived in Houston, Texas, Moroni Stone, read my blessing and told me that my blessing said my children would hold the priesthood. "Where does it say that?" I questioned him. "Right here, in your addendum," he said as he pointed to it in my blessing. I looked at my blessing, read it, and looked up at him. As I had read it in the past, I understood it to mean I would have sons. Patriarch Stone said yes, and that they would hold the priesthood.

My blessing was given in February 1978, just four months prior to the revelation stating that "every worthy male" could hold the priesthood, or Official Declaration 2, as it is now known. The Lord knew what was in store, but my eyes weren't opened to see it in my own blessing until much later. Years later, my husband would comment, "Isn't it interesting that your blessing would say this, and all our sons are adopted?" The Lord knew well in advance that we would have sons and that those sons would hold the priesthood.

I didn't push going on a mission after that, at least not until four months later. June 8, 1978, started out as any other day. I was home from school at my parent's house in Detroit. In the afternoon I heard a national news break that said, "President Spencer W. Kimball of the Mormon Church has announced that Blacks can now hold the priesthood." I stopped in my tracks. What? Is this a joke? Is he serious? Whom can I call? Brother Stamps? He was my home teacher, but that would be a long-distance call. This could be a wild rumor. "Wait," I thought, "if this is really from the Lord, He will tell me himself."

I walked into my bedroom, closed the door, and knelt down. My heart was pounding. I began my prayer, "Heavenly Father, I just heard something on the news. Is it true?" Before I could finish my thoughts, my whole bosom began to burn. My whole body seemed to burn from within. It was true! "Does this mean I can go on a mission?" I inquired.

"Yes," came the reply. I uttered "thank you" over and over again. I promised the Lord that I would serve Him on a mission. I stood up with tears in my eyes. The burning in my bosom lasted the rest of the day.

I learned early on, in my spiritual growth, not to lean on or depend on my own understanding. As I searched the scriptures diligently, prayed always, and believed that I would receive an answer to my prayers, I often did. Not always immediately, but just when I needed the reassurance, He was there.

CHAPTER THREE

My God is an On Time God

"If any of you lack wisdom, let him ask of God,
that giveth to all men liberally, and upbraideth not;
and it shall be given him."

—JAMES 1:5

After June 1978 I focused on and worked toward
my goal of serving a full-time mission. I graduated from
college in August 1979 and immediately submitted my
paperwork for a mission call. Then I waited. I waited a
long time. Nothing came. Finally I called my bishop and
was told that my paperwork had not been sent to Salt Lake
City yet because I was not old enough to serve a mission.
I had graduated from college six months before I turned
twenty-one. My papers could not be submitted more than
ninety days before I turned twenty-one. Bummer. I had
to wait some more.

While I waited, I started to prepare. Being a new

member of the church, I didn't have any background on how to do this. Regardless, I read everything I could and made sure I had read through all of the standard works at least once. I studied the *Gospel Principles* manual a couple of times, marking every scripture cited in my set of scriptures. I asked people what missionaries should read before and during a mission, and I read and studied those books. Finally, after I had done all I could to prepare, I went to the Lord in prayer and asked Him what I should do to prepare for my mission.

His answer came quite clearly, "Complete your four generations."

"What?" I thought. "What does my genealogy have to do with a mission?" Since the answer didn't make any sense, I asked again, "Heavenly Father, what do I need to do to prepare for a mission?"

Again, the answer was just as clear as before, "Complete your four generations." About this time, President Spencer W. Kimball had asked and encouraged every member to research, complete, and submit four generations of his or her family history, so I knew what the Lord was referring to. Still, I thought to myself, "I could do that anytime or when I get back from a mission." Right now, I wanted to know what I should do to prepare for a proselyting mission, not my life's mission. Being the only member of the Church in my family, I didn't have any knowledge or background about how to prepare for a mission. I had faith that if I did all I could, Heavenly Father would certainly help me know how to get ready. Maybe I wasn't asking the question correctly. I tried rewording my prayer to get Heavenly Father to understand what I was asking. But no matter how I worded my prayer, no matter what I said, He kept giving one and only one response: "Complete your four generations."

"Okay," I thought to myself, "I give up. I'll just copy the four generations onto a family group sheet, and family record and be done with it." So I did. My mother and Aunt Terry had given me some genealogy, so I just copied it onto some forms with the Church's copyright symbol on them, because I thought that was what the Lord wanted me to do, and placed it in front of me before I knelt down in prayer.

"Heavenly Father, I've completed the four generations you told me to do. Now, what do I need to do to prepare for a mission?"

"Verify it," came His reply.

"Oh, it's correct. My aunt Terry did this research and gave it to me," I assured Him.

"Verify it," came His reply.

From previous experience, I knew I wouldn't get any other reply until I did what He told me to do. So I went to my mother and told her we should verify all our family history information. We, along with my Aunt Terry, planned a trip to Dresden, Ontario, Canada—just a quick trip from Detroit, across the border, to verify her family's information.

As I packed for our trip, I packed a copy of the missionary discussions to take along with me, so I could continue to memorize them. I just knew if I could get the Lord to understand what I was asking, about how to prepare for a mission, He would tell me to memorize the discussions in preparation to enter the Missionary Training Center (MTC). I knew I wasn't expected to learn the discussions before entering in the MTC. But I thought if I studied them and memorized them prior to entering the MTC, I could skip the MTC to get right down to business and teach the gospel.

We had some official certificates to verify information, but we were really just filling in the gaps and looking for siblings of our descendants. While in Dresden, we met Arlie C. Robbins, a distant relative, who spent all her spare time doing genealogy. She was hampered with arthritis, but was still a wealth of information. We visited with her in her home.

As we were talking, my mother told Arlie that I "was preparing to go on a mission for the Mormon Church."

"The Mormons?" she said with surprise. "Why, did you know there was one of those in our family?"

My ears perked up, "No, I didn't."

"Why, yes, there was a Mormon and when they found out he was Black, they took his priesthood from him." Right then and there I knew that could only be the LDS Church.

She told us the name, and we learned that this Latter-day Saint ancestor was a brother to my direct ancestor in the Richardson line. Arlie then said, just as seriously, "I guess that bad blood just stayed dormant until you." I just smiled, now knowing I had an ancestor in the LDS Church. What a find!

We continued our research and attempted to find some cemeteries around the area. One store clerk said, "The cemeteries *you* want" are located along such and such a road. His emphasis on the cemeteries we wanted was because back then, Black and Whites were not buried together. We found a cemetery or two, but we could not read the headstones clearly.

Still, our trip was worth it. We found we had mixed up a generation, thinking two individuals were father and son when they were in fact brothers. It was a good thing we verified the records we had. Had it not been for the Lord telling me to verify the records, I would have left well enough alone.

After we returned home, I continued to wait for a mission call. Finally, it came. I had been called to serve

in the Texas Houston Mission. I knelt down to thank the
Lord for sending me there—after looking at a map to see
where Houston was located. I was excited. Finally, I was
really going on a mission. The Lord wanted me to go. I
wanted to go. I was ready to go.

I flew out to Salt Lake City alone. I arrived a day
before my scheduled check-in, and so I actually had my
first night to myself—no companion yet. I asked at the front
desk what there was to do nearby that I could walk to. She
told me about the BYU campus and gave me directions.
I walked over to the campus and found the student center
in the Wilkinson building. I sat down to watch "Eight is
Enough" on TV, but I didn't feel comfortable. I left there
and walked over to the Harold B. Lee Library. As I looked
around, I learned the library had a genealogy floor. I went
to the fourth floor just to look up a name or two.

Because I had just spent so much time in Canada
copying group and family sheets, I knew some names and
dates off the top of my head. I looked up the Richardson
name to find the ancestor who was supposed to have been
LDS. I found his records immediately.

I wrote down the name of the person who submitted
the information and noted that he lived in Baytown,
Texas. I wondered if that was anywhere near Houston. All
the temple work had been done, and I thought to myself,
it was a good thing I had done that research. Who knows

when I would have run across this information?

When I arrived in Houston, I asked my trainer/companion, Sister Joan Oka (now Hesley), where Baytown was located. She said it was right across the bay from where we were in La Porte. It wasn't even a long-distance phone call. I told her about having a distant relative who was LDS, and called the person who submitted the information to the Church's genealogy library. When I called, I told the man who answered the phone that I thought I was related to the Richardsons.

He said, "These aren't the Richardsons you're looking for. These are Black."

"Those are the Richardson's I'm looking for," I assured him. "I'm Black, and I'm the first Black missionary to come to Houston. I'm a distant relative to the Richardson who joined the Church in the 1800s in Canada." I asked if all the information he had, had been submitted to the Church. It had. I thanked him for his time and hung up.

"Boy, it's a good thing I completed my four generations before I left," I thought, "or I wouldn't have found out about this gentleman and had a chance to talk with him." I also thought that was the end of the genealogy connection on my mission—but it wasn't.

While in my next area, I met a member, Brother Perry, who grew up near Dresden, Ontario. I told him about my trip there to research my family history and some of

the stumbling blocks we ran into, such as not being able
to read headstones. He leaned forward and asked for my
family names. I told him some names, and he reached for
a piece of paper and began to draw a map. As he drew, he
told me that as a boy he used to play in those cemeteries
where Blacks were buried, and for whatever reason, he
still had the headstones memorized. He handed me a map
of the cemeteries, detailing headstone locations where
some of my ancestors were buried.

"Wow," I thought, "it's a good thing I knew about the
relatives up in Canada and had attempted to locate the
cemeteries."

From my last area, I called my "distant relative" in
Baytown, Texas, to say good-bye before leaving the state.
I spoke with his daughter, who told me he had died a
few months ago. I expressed my sympathy and hung up.
Timing is everything, I thought.

In Isaiah 55:8–9, the Lord says, "Behold my thoughts
are not your thoughts, neither are your ways my ways, saith
the Lord. For as the heavens are higher than the earth, so
are my ways higher than your ways, and my thoughts than
your thoughts." As I look back on my prayers about my
mission preparation before leaving for Texas, I realize that
Heavenly Father's answer did not make any sense at the
time, but I'm glad I followed His instructions. As events
unfolded, His wisdom or "His ways" became evident. Had

I not listened and completed my four generations before I left on a mission, I would not have known about distant relatives in the Church who were Black, nor would I have had the map Brother Perry drew for me.

I am in awe of the Lord's orchestration in preparing the way for these advances in my family history research—and it wasn't even my focus. I'm sure the hardest part for the Lord was getting me to do the four generations *before* I left on a mission. His inspiration and guidance saw to it that I received a mission call to Houston, Texas. Now, who can doubt that the prophet and brethren are inspired of the Lord when mission calls are issued? The Lord's inspiration and guidance saw to it that a young boy would not only play in a remote cemetery in Dresden, Canada but that the boy would retain those memories and would be able to draw a map decades later that would include the names on the headstones. God is good!

Years later, I realized my family history experience was not the only long drawn out answer from the Lord played out during my eighteen-month mission. During this time, I couldn't help but notice much of my time was spent with elderly companions. Because I was told our mission had more sister missionaries than any other mission in the world, I thought it unfair that I was with older sisters so much. Surely, there were some young sisters I could be paired with. I talked with my mission president about my concerns and on the next transfer, I was again paired with an elderly companion. Each month at transfer I was disappointed and became depressed. I would go into my closet, literally, and pour my heart and soul out to the Lord.

"Why am I still with an older sister?" I'd ask.

Those prayers went unanswered for four years, until one afternoon in 1985. Four years after I returned from my mission, I was sitting in a hospital room with my mother when I once again heard the Lord's voice.

"Do you remember asking me why you were with older companions so much during your mission?" I heard.

Startled, I looked all around to see who was talking. I looked in the empty bed on the other side of my mother's room. I was sitting with my back to my mother, and I turned and looked at her. She was still unconscious and motionless. I leaned forward in my chair and looked out in the hallway to see if I could see anyone. I saw no one.

Not knowing where else to look; I looked up and said, "What?"

"Do you remember asking me why you were with older companions so much during your mission?" I heard once again.

"Yes."

"It was so, that when you reached this point in your

life, you would have the patience and know-how to take care of your mother when she reached this point in her life."

My eyes filled with tears because I knew exactly what He was talking about.

The Lord finally answered the prayer I had uttered years before. Again, I am in awe of the Lord's care in preparing the way for me to take care of my mother at her time of need. My mission president, Kay Clifford, followed the inspiration of the Lord as he oversaw each transfer in the mission field that involved me. Surely He saw to it that each companion I needed to learn from was sent to the same mission to give me certain experiences. The Lord knew the future and prepared me for what was to come.

Although it took five years to receive an answer to my prayers, I literally heard an answer, and that answer came right on time. This experience brings to my mind the words of a Black gospel song: "He's an on time God, yes He is. He may not come when you want Him to, but He'll be there right on time. He's an on time God, yes He is."

CHAPTER FOUR

Choosing a Husband

"Trust in the Lord with all thine heart; and lean
not unto thine own understanding. In all thy ways
acknowledge him, and he shall direct thy paths."

—PROVERBS 3:5-6

During my mission, when the stake patriarch, Moroni Stone, reviewed my blessing, he said something else of significance, besides that my sons would hold the priesthood. As he looked over my blessing, he asked what I intended to do after my mission. I gave the standard pat answers about wanting to get married, maybe going on to graduate school, and anything else I thought he wanted to hear. He looked at me and back to my blessing and said, "Well you go on to graduate school, travel, or work because you aren't going to get married until you are twenty-six or twenty-seven years old." I almost fell off my chair. I was twenty-two years old and near the end of my mission. "Not until I was *that old*?" I thought to myself. He continued, "Yes, you continue on with whatever you plan to do. And I will tell you something else, he will not choose you, you will choose him." Because such information was not actually in my blessing, I didn't know how much credibility to give it.

After I returned home from my mission, I applied to BYU for graduate school in English. I was accepted and planned to attend in the fall of 1983. As I was planning the trip out west, I learned of a young BYU student, who lived in my stake, who was looking for a ride to Provo, Utah. I called her and we talked to get to know one another. When she asked how old I was, I told her—twenty-four. "Twenty-four? You're that old, a return missionary, and you're not married?" Oh no, it's true I thought to myself. Everyone in Utah is married by time they are my age. I'm an old maid by Utah standards. I got cold feet about going out to Utah, but still I went.

While in Utah, I occasionally went to The Genesis Group meetings in Salt Lake City. At one meeting, I listened to a man bear his testimony, and I thought to myself that he was really good-looking. At a later meeting, my brother Jacob, who had joined the Church by now, and I were leaving and as we said good-bye to Betty Bridgeforth, as a courtesy and not to appear rude by ignoring him, I introduced myself to the man standing next to her—the same good-looking man I took note of in a previous meeting. Some time later, I was invited to an open house or party of some kind, to be held where else but at the home of the "good-looking man" who attended Genesis. I had planned to attend, but backed out at the last minute, because I had so much work to do.

In January 1985, I attended a program on campus that was put on by The Genesis Group. Soon after I arrived and took a seat, a man approached me and introduced himself. It was none other than Alan Cherry, whom I had often corresponded with while I was on my mission. We had never met until that night. He sat down next to me, and we watched the program. After the program ended, several people wanted to meet Alan and get their picture taken with him.

I didn't want to stand around and be bored so I decided to go up front and introduce myself to some of the people I did not know. I started in the left corner with a "good-looking man"who was sitting off by himself and who had served as the Master of Ceremonies for the program.

I introduced myself to Don Harwell, and many others that night. After talking a little, Don asked me out to dinner that evening and I accepted. How old was I when I met him? I met Don about six weeks before I turned twenty-six!

We dated for several months, but in June, I left Utah to attend the Radcliffe Publishing Procedures Course in Cambridge, Massachusetts. I had applied to the program a few years earlier and I was not accepted. Not being one to give up easily, I called the director of the program and told him I had applied to the program and I was not accepted. I was calling to find out why I was not accepted. What skills or abilities did the other candidates have that I did not? What can I work on to increase my chances of being accepted when I apply again? The director told me, and I worked to develop those skills and I applied a second time. This time, of course, I was successful.

When I left Utah, I stored all my belongings at Don's house, because I had planned to return in the fall. While at Radcliffe, I received a "Dear Jane" letter from Don. He had met someone else, and was moving on. I was hurt, angry, and livid. How dare he dump me! With his letter in hand, I took off one weekend to drive through several of the New England states. I drove up to Maine, through New Hampshire, and into Vermont to visit Brigham Young's birthplace. I came back into western Massachusetts and headed back to Cambridge.

While driving, I kept playing a song by El DeBarge titled, "Who's Holding Donna Now?" I kept hearing "Donald" in place of Donna, but you get the message. I was crying over Don's letter and half-heartedly praying

to Heavenly Father. Out of the blue, I heard that
familiar voice.

"Are you in love with him?"

"Uh, no," I answered.

"When you return to Utah in the fall, would you
have wanted to marry him?"

"No, not really" I had to answer in all honesty.

"If you ever want a chance with him, leave him alone
for now."

"Hey, what am I supposed to do, wait for the broad
to die?"

"If you ever want a chance with him, leave him alone
for now," came the same response.

Thinking over all the thoughts I had and the hurt
feelings, I realized it was only my pride that had been
hurt. I wasn't even in love with this guy.

I finished the publishing program and returned home
to Detroit. While away for the summer, I knew my mother
had been in the hospital, but I did not know how serious
her condition was until I returned home. My father did
not want me to know so I would not quit the publishing
program and come home early. My mother had had a
series of heart attacks and had suffered brain damage. I
decided not to return to BYU in the fall, but instead I
would stay home to care for my mother, who would need
assistance twenty-four hours a day. I drove out to Utah to

collect my things from Don's house. I said good-bye and thought that was the end of that relationship.

Within weeks of my returning home, my mother died. Still, it was a good thing I stayed home, because ten days before my mother died, my father had a stroke and was in the same hospital my mother was in when she died. I was home to care for my father and still I was making progress on my graduate degree. I was taking classes at Wayne State University in Detroit, completing extra work, and transferring the credit to BYU. I didn't date while I was in Detroit. I really just biding my time, fighting bouts of depression, and waiting until I could return to Utah.

I did return to Provo and BYU in the fall of 1986. About this time, I started thinking more and more about marriage. I was getting older and I was ready to move onto the next stage of life. I was not dating anyone but I remember talking to Heavenly Father about the subject in prayer. I told Him I wanted to get married, and during one of these prayers he asked, "And why do you want to get married?" Knowing He knows all of my thoughts before I even ask Him, what good would it do to beat around the bush? As Bishop H. Burke Peterson counseled, I knew I should tell him things I really felt—not trite phrases that have little meaning. I truly wanted a heartfelt conversation with him. I should confide in Him.

So I did, and I said, "Because I want to have [intimate

relations of a physical nature]," I confided, with some embarrassment. At that point He laughed and said, "Come back to me when you have a better reason."

It took me a few weeks to come up with a better reason or reasons. I knelt down in prayer and began, "Heavenly Father, I came to you a few weeks ago and talked about how I wanted to get married. I still want to have [intimate relations], but also I feel I have progressed as far as I can in life as a single woman and achieved most of the goals I had set for myself. I'm almost finished with graduate school, I've traveled, and I've done everything I've wanted to do up to this point in my life. Now my goals need to focus on someone else besides me. I need the challenges and experiences that come with a husband and children." I waited and listened. Nothing. I felt nothing. I heard nothing. "Oh well," I thought, "that's how I honestly feel and if it's not reason enough, then it's not reason enough."

I focused on other things over the next several weeks. In fact, I had actually contacted Don again. While I was in Detroit, I noticed that I was missing a book that I had stored at Don's house. It was a leatherbound copy of *Jesus the Christ* and *The Articles of Faith* by James E. Talmage, with my name engraved on the front of it. I assumed Don had pulled it out of my boxes of books to read while my things were stored at his house.

About this time a friend, Susan Frampton, told me she saw Don at a grocery store and noticed that he didn't have a wedding band on. We speculated about his marital state. Soon afterward, I looked up his work number and called and left a message for him. He returned my call and I asked him if by chance he had the book. He did. He said he found it in his closet and had kept it. He didn't know how it got separated from my things because he had not removed it to read.

We arranged for me to pick it up the next weekend. I drove to his apartment to pick up the book. When I arrived, he was moving a TV to make room for a new one he had purchased. I mentioned that I was renting a television while in school. He offered for me to use his old one instead of paying rent. I took him up on his offer because I thought it would give me at least one more opportunity to see him—when I returned the TV at the end of the year.

Soon enough he was calling and we talked on the phone a great deal. We went out occasionally, usually on Wednesday afternoons when he was in the Provo/Orem area on sales calls. Just before Valentine's Day that year, it suddenly occurred to me that I was seeing four different men that I had the opportunity to date.

One man was a member and prospering financially. Another was also a member but he was not doing well financially. A third was financially well-off, but he was not a member. Then there was Don. "What a choice," I found myself thinking one day. Suddenly a light went off in my mind. Within six weeks, I had gone from dating no one to dating four different men. I thought of my prayers about wanting to get married. The Lord had not verbally answered, but He answered by putting several choices before me. I also recalled the words of the stake patriarch, Moroni Stone, years before, ". . . he will not choose you, you will choose him."

The weekend around Valentine's Day, I went out with all four men, two of them in one day. Don was not the one I was in love with but he was definitely the one I had the most fun with, and the one I enjoyed being with the most.

Once again, not wanting to set myself up to be hurt, I didn't say anything to him. We were good friends and usually discussed our dates with each other. Soon I couldn't help but notice that it bothered me to hear him talk about the other women he was dating. "Why would that be?" I asked myself. The answer was obvious. I was falling in love with him.

Now the word "love," according to Don, is the most often abused word in history. People use it without even knowing what it means. He always felt having a friendship with your partner was more important than "being in love." It's more important to "be in like, than in love. When the allure of the physical attraction wears off, you had better really like the person you are still married to and with whom you wake up to each morning."

One evening Don called, as he did just about every night. "So, what did you do today?" he asked me. Nonchalantly, and really without any thought, I told him, "I sent off about twenty-nine letters of inquiry about Ph.D. programs around the country."

"You're leaving Utah? What about us?" he asked.

Not knowing he was serious, I responded, "Us? I didn't know there was an us to plan my life around."

Within a few weeks, there was! We discussed marriage and looked at homes to buy. He never did actually propose to me. While driving around looking at homes, he asked me if I wanted an engagement ring or would I like to use the money for a down payment on a house. Knowing jewelry rarely appreciates in value, but homes almost always do appreciate, I told him I'd like to put the money toward the down payment on a house. That decision has paid off many times over.

That same summer, my sister, Odessa, made plans to get married in June. She invited me to join in on her plans and have a double wedding. Our mutual friends and family would be in Maryland for her wedding. I declined. Although she had joined the Church, she was marrying a nonmember and her bishop was performing the ceremony. I opted for a temple sealing. Don and I flew to Maryland for her wedding. This also presented an opportunity for my family to meet him.

We made plans to get married in August, after the semester ended. When we found a home in July, we moved our wedding date up, thinking we would just move right in. (It actually took five months to close on the home.) Don insisted we get married on a Monday, "because the sealing rooms aren't full like they are on a Saturday." He was right. There was only one other bride in the bridal area while I was there. Don and I were married July 20, 1987, in the Salt Lake Temple, exactly one month after my sister and her husband Eddie.

Don and I often discuss the leatherbound book that found its way out of my boxes while in storage. He had never removed it. No one else would have had a reason to remove it. We really feel the Lord had a part in it, just so I would have a reason to contact Don again and so we could resume the relationship. He directed our paths and guided us into an eternal marriage.

CHAPTER FIVE

Church and Community Service by Inspiration

". . . when ye are in the service of your fellow beings
ye are only in the service of your God."

—MOSIAH 2:17

After my husband Don and I were married, we soon learned I was unable to have children. We knew why— I had a cyst on my pituitary gland, which threw my hormone levels off just enough that I could not conceive. We weighed the pros and cons of infertility treatments and decided the monetary costs were too high, considering nothing was guaranteed. Before we got married, we had discussed having our own children and adopting. Since I couldn't conceive, and fertility treatments weren't guaranteed, we decided to adopt. We knew children were out there waiting to be adopted, and we thought we could offer them a chance at a good life. Little did we know how quickly that would happen.

It all started in May 1990 when a phone call from a friend informed us a child in foster care needed another home immediately. Although we had planned to adopt children since before we were married, we had never considered foster care.

So we quickly thought about foster care and its inherent potential to adopt the child later on. Less than forty-eight hours from the time we heard about Christopher, he was in our home. Two days later, the state conducted a home study, and we became a licensed foster care home. Again, we weren't interested in being foster care parents unless we could adopt the children. Our objective was to provide these kids with a chance to have a good home. We wanted them to have some stability and security.

Chris turned seven years old just after we got him. When he came to live with us, he couldn't say the whole alphabet, much less write it. I was determined to have him in a mainstream class in school, so I took it upon myself to teach him how to read. I worked with him for one hour a day and taught him how to read. It worked. In the fall, he tested on grade level. The school psychologist and his teacher were amazed considering his background three and a half months before.

Also during that summer, I was informed about a possible private adoption of a newborn. It fell through, or so I thought. One day, I received a phone call asking if my husband and I would still consider adopting a newborn (the same one I had been trying to follow up on all summer). I said yes to the person on the phone, took Chris to school, and went to work at Don's office. After I left the house that morning, Don received a phone call from the state's Department of Family Services letting him know that we could have two- and four-year-old brothers on a foster care to adopt basis.

He said, "Yes, we'll do it."

It was not until we got together that afternoon and talked that we realized we had committed to three kids in one day! As it turned out, the baby, now known as Morgan Lyle, was born two weeks early. On the day his birth mother was scheduled to have a C-section, Don was out of town elk hunting. By "out of town," I mean a three-and-a-half hour drive to the high Unitas and another three-and-a-half hour hike into a base camp. There was no way to contact him to let him know Morgan had been born. With our attorney's counsel, I made the decision to take custody of Morgan, even though Don didn't know anything about him being born.

The day after making the decision, I went shopping to buy everything a baby would need for its first week of life.

My intentions were to bring the baby home and wait for Don to come home five days later. Because I didn't have the slightest idea what to do with a newborn, my oldest sister, LaClaire, had planned to fly to Utah to stay with me at least until Don came home. None of that turned out to be necessary.

When I learned the baby had been born early, I was scared about bringing him home and taking care of him all by myself. I knelt down and prayed. I told Heavenly Father that Don was out hunting and unreachable except by Him. I said I didn't mean to use Him as a messenger service, but if there was any way He could touch Don's heart and inspire Don to come home, I would appreciate it. Because Don had planned this trip for months and had taken two or three dry runs up to the base camp, I knew he wouldn't come home until he had an elk or the hunting season ended. The day after the hunt began, Don walked in the door—and without an elk. I told him that the baby had been born early and that we were going to pick him up the next day, if he were released.

Don, the good-hearted man that he is simply said, "Okay." I then asked why he came home early, and he said, "I don't know. I just felt I had to get home right away because you needed me." Surely the Lord touched his heart and got the message to him that his family needed him at home.

We were able to pick up Morgan from the hospital on October 6, 1990, when he was just four days old. Our good friend Reba Stoney (now Johnson) went with us. Because the placement worker at the Department of Family Services, Steven Klein, was concerned about how I would handle a newborn and the other two boys all at once, we all decided it was best to wait six weeks before bringing Ricky and Ronnie into our home. Finally, on November 17, we picked up Ricky and Ronnie from their foster parents, Lynne (now Cuff) and Bill Nebeker. At the finalization of the adoptions, we changed their names to Richard and Bronson. We had gone from zero to four kids in six months!

In Utah, we had to wait six months before we could finalize the adoptions. We changed Morgan's venue, or jurisdiction, to our local county so we could finalize all the adoptions at once in the same county. By this time Chris had left our home supposedly to go live with relatives who wanted him.

Now that we had the three boys, I hadn't been consciously trying to get pregnant, but one night I was praying about having more children. I asked the Lord if we were going to have more children and He said, "Yes."

I then asked, "Are we going to adopt another child?"

"No, not necessarily," came the response.

I got up and told Don that we were going to have another child and that we wouldn't have to adopt him or her. Because he was sleeping, his only reply was a grunt. I was so excited I could hardly sleep. Two weeks later, my menstrual cycle began and I knew I wasn't pregnant. I started to get depressed again, but I knew what I heard the Lord say and I knew I just had to be patient. The next month, when my menstrual cycle was one day late, I knew I was pregnant. My doctor confirmed it. Just three weeks before our court date to finalize the adoptions, I learned I was pregnant!

Being afraid the judge wouldn't grant all the adoptions if he knew I was finally able to get pregnant, I didn't say a word about it when we went into Judge Michael Murphy's chambers. I thought I had invented the "Don't ask, don't tell" policy. Our adoptions went through and we had an instant family with one more on the way.

During one prayer, I felt that the spirits we adopted were the spirits that would have been born to us had we gotten married soon after we first met. Once again, I recalled the words of the stake patriarch, Moroni Stone, years before, "Well you go on to graduate school, travel, or work because you aren't going to get married until you are twenty-six or twenty-seven years old." I met Don, in 1985, about six weeks before I turned twenty-six. Had we gotten married in 1985, our oldest son, who was born in November 1986, could very well have been born into that union.

I was twenty-eight when we got married, but then I thought about the decisions we made that kept us apart. We certainly used and exercised our free agency, but the Lord orchestrated our lives, to be sure we ended up together despite our choices. He even made sure we ended up "with the spirits that would have been born to us, had we gotten married when we first met."

Our daughter Rene Allene was born February 7, 1992. Both my sister, LaClaire, and my brother, Jacob, came out to help after she was born. Despite their help, our ward bishopric felt Don and I were overwhelmed with the instant family and our Church callings. One evening the bishop and one of his counselors came over to our house and told us they wanted to help us out, so they were releasing us from all of our callings. I was devastated. Just when I needed anything outside of the kids to focus on, it was taken from me. I told the bishop that I didn't feel it was right for him to make a decision for my family without consulting us. Don began to roll his eyes because he knew I had never been one to mince words. I told the men that they had no idea if family was helping out or if we were hiring a nanny—not that we really had the money mind you—but my point was they did not consult us or ask if we wanted to be released.

That period of time was one of the hardest trials of my faith. Don and I discussed going inactive in the Church merely because we had nothing to do. It was so much easier to stay home with the kids when the time for church rolled around, and I often did. I was not happy. I was not giving of myself to others and I felt a loss. While praying, I poured out my heart to Heavenly Father and told Him how I didn't have anything to do in the Church and I didn't know what to do about it. He replied, "I never said Church service only had to be among Church members."

"What?"

"I never said Church service only had to be among Church members," he repeated. I looked up the scriptures and read Mosiah 2:17, about service and read it over and over. It read in part, "When ye are in the service of your fellow beings ye are only in the service of your God."

"Well, since I'm not wanted in Church for any kind of service or calling," I thought to myself "I'll just go out into the community and volunteer. I also realized this might even help me fulfill part of my patriarchal blessing, which reads, "He will bless [me] with intelligence and leadership qualities that [I] may be influential in the church and also in [my] community." Within the next week or two after that prayer, I received a notice about Black business owners getting together. I found a sitter and attended. After the meeting, a woman approached me about attending another meeting to organize a Black woman's coalition in the Salt Lake area. I attended that organizational meeting and many other meetings over the next several months. I was one of the founding members and first officers in the Utah Coalition of African-American Women. Next I worked with Black business owners and became one of the founding members and first officers in the Utah Black Business Entrepreneurs, helping develop and write the bylaws for those organizations also.

About this time, I also approached Ruffin Bridgeforth, then president of The Genesis Group—the Church's official auxiliary for Black Latter-day Saints—with the idea of a newsletter. I didn't just outline it; I came up with a logo, design, and text. I then presented him with the idea and first issue. He loved it and said, "With this, I know we can't fail."

That newsletter was published and sent out around the world, with the Church printing 1,700 copies a month. I laugh when I think about my late nights putting the newsletter together, running copies at a local copy store, folding, stuffing, and licking each envelope, and putting on each label and stamp monthly. I didn't even think to ask anyone to help with the costs. I considered it service to my God and "my fellow beings."

Once I even spoke before a group of Black ministers

in the region to discuss the goals and purpose of the Utah Coalition of African-American Women. One minister told me I was living a lie being a Black member of the LDS Church.

I simply said, "That's your opinion," and moved on. After the meeting, another minister came up to me and apologized for what the first minister had said in front of everyone and said he had no right to do that. I said he was merely expressing his opinion and that I didn't agree with him, but I wasn't going to argue with him either. After that I became known in the Black community as "that Mormon lady."

Another woman came up to me after the same meeting and told me how impressed she was with my presentation and that I held my own "with that minister." She also complimented me on my leadership skills. Leadership skills. That's what my patriarchal blessing talked about, and I had put it out of my mind. Surely the Lord's hand was involved in pushing me out into my community to work and serve Him.

Not too long ago I was thinking about my patriarchal blessing while working as a librarian in my ward and also the ward newsletter editor. It felt good to be useful. Still, I sat and pondered my role of being "influential in the church and community" as a ward librarian. While sitting in on a ward correlation meeting one Sunday so I could get dates for the ward newsletter, I heard someone in the bishopric say it was time to reorganize the Relief Society. Then I heard a voice say, "And you will be in the presidency."

"You mean I'm going to be Relief Society President?" I asked in my mind.

"No, but you're going to be in the presidency," the voice said again. I put the thought out of my mind because I didn't like Relief Society.

I didn't think about it again until I was called into the Bishop Paul Nance's office just a few short months later and asked to be a counselor in the ward's Relief Society presidency. I looked right at the bishop and without hesitation, said, "Look, I don't ever want to be considered a hypocrite. I don't like Relief Society and I never have. I can't be in the presidency, so no. I'm not going to stand up in meetings talking about how much I love Relief Society. I don't, and I won't put on airs and pretend I do."

The bishop and his counselor questioned me about why I didn't like it. Maybe *I* could be the one to affect change, they reasoned, but I still said no. They tried their best to get me to accept the calling but I was not interested. After I left the office, I walked toward the cultural hall to get my kids. Suddenly my chest felt as if someone had stopped me by hitting me with a fist.

"Go back in there and undo that," I heard.

I knew who it was and I knew what He was talking about, but I didn't want to serve in that position, so I looked back down the hall and said, "The door is closed, and they're meeting with someone else now."

"That's okay, they have to come out to go home, and you can talk to them then."

I then asked why I had to be in Relief Society.

He replied, "Because there will be people who will walk into that room in the next two years that you need to be there for." I ignored the voice, got my kids, and went home.

As I pulled in front of my house, I was consciously talking to the Lord and telling Him that I wasn't going back because I didn't want that calling.

He then said, "It's not always about what you want." I felt so bad that I immediately called Darius Gray, then president of The Genesis Group, from my cell phone and told him what happened. He told me I needed to accept the calling. I told him I knew that, but I really didn't want to accept it. Next, I called my husband. I told him what had happened, and he said, "I think you need to accept the calling. Go back and tell them you'll accept it."

I went into my house, but I literally could not sit down. I told my kids I had to go back over to the church building and I left. I sat outside the bishop's door until it opened. The bishop said good-bye to the person leaving,

and I stood up and humbly asked if I could undo my
earlier decision. Bishop Nance looked surprised and
invited me in. Everyone who had been there an hour
earlier was still there. I told them I'd like to accept the
calling, and they allowed me to. One counselor, John
Hamren, asked what changed my mind. "The Spirit," I
answered, and left it at that.

When I spoke with Leigh Gallimore, the newly called
Relief Society president, I told her the whole story. I
wanted no misunderstandings about how I felt, and she
needed to know that I only accepted the calling after
much persuasion from the Lord. She laughed and told me
about her experience with her calling. She also related that
she had received the prompting, some time earlier, that
she would "be called to be the Relief Society President
and Jerri Harwell will be one of your counselors." Once
again, I'm sure the hardest part of the Lord putting all this
together was getting *me* to accept the calling.

Once I accepted the calling, I still needed the Lord's
help to change my attitude. I learned that sometimes it
means more to just be there for people than to lead and
direct. For example, one evening I was having a hard
time making myself go to Enrichment night. I asked the
Lord if it was worth it for me to go. "I'm tired. I'm not
interested. I just don't want to go. You said there were
people I had to be there for, and I haven't met anyone."

I left for Enrichment, arrived late, and ate dinner. As I left the cultural hall to go to a class, I turned around and looked back into the room just as a sister was coming out. As I looked at her, I heard the Lord's voice: "And here comes one of them now." She introduced herself to me and said maybe her daughter would have come had the daughter (who was Black) known I, being a Black member of the Church, would be there. Humbly, I make sure I'm at every meeting I'm suppose to be to now, *especially* when I don't feel like it.

A similar incident occurred within two weeks of being called to work in Relief Society. My daughter's principal asked me to be PTA president at her elementary school. I weighed the decision and time commitment. I even took a chance to pray about it. The Lord told me to take the position "because there will be people in halls you will need to talk to when they are there." I accepted the position in addition to having been reelected to the Cottonwood Heights Community Council the previous fall. I felt overwhelmed. I was expressing my concerns to President Darius Gray, then President of the Genesis Group, while we were sitting in the celestial room in the Jordan River Temple. He said a prayer with me, and in that prayer, blessed me that I would be able to handle all the new responsibilities. We spoke of my patriarchal blessing, and I asked him, as I had asked the Lord, why I had so many leadership responsibilities at once. We never got a clear answer on that one—yet.

Still I do not lean on my own understanding. I lean on the Lord for support, guidance, and endurance. One thing I do clearly understand, is that my responsibility in this life is to be of service to my God, however that may fit into His plans, not mine.

CHAPTER SIX

For the Glory of God

"Search diligently, pray always, and be believing,
and all things shall work together for your good."
—DOCTRINE AND COVENANTS 90:24

Lest anyone thinks, after reading these experiences, that I hear verbal answers to all of my prayers, let me state for the record that I don't. In fact, very few of my prayers are answered audibly. Often I feel a burning. Sometimes my prayers are answered through other people. Most aren't answered at all—yet.

Most of the answers are straightforward and poignant. Others have served as a wake-up call. Once when I prayed and asked if there was anything I could do to further the Lord's work, Heavenly Father told me to call someone. I got up from my knees, crawled into bed, and forgot about it. A couple of days later, I remembered the prayer, but I couldn't remember who I was supposed to call.

I figured if the Lord told me once, He'd tell me again. I knelt in prayer and asked whom I was suppose to call. His immediate response was, "I've already gotten someone else to do it. If I had wanted you to wait two days to call, I would have waited two days to tell you to call." I'll never know the opportunity I missed from not remembering and acting on that prayer.

Of course, I still learn something from each lesson on prayer I hear. While attending BYU years ago, I took to heart a lesson and prayed to know whom I could help during the next week. That week while driving home, I saw a lady in a wheelchair waiting at some railroad tracks. I had seen her there before, and I just thought she liked to watch the trains going by. However, during the week of my specific prayer to help someone, I saw her again. I heard a voice that said, "Stop and help her."

"Oh she doesn't need any help. She likes like to look at trains," I thought to myself, trying to dismiss the voice.

"Stop and help her," I heard again. I pulled my car over, and walked over to her, hoping she didn't think I was too weird.

"Do you need some help?" I asked.

"Yes, I do," she answered. "I'm trying to cross the tracks, but my front wheels get stuck, and I have to sit and wait until someone stops to help me."

Hoping she didn't see the tears of humility in my

eyes, I lifted her front wheels across the tracks and she was gone. I lived in that part of town for several months, and I often looked for her as I crossed the tracks. I never did see her again.

Once I felt I received instruction from the Lord in a dream. I was living with my father, in Michigan, for several months after my mother died, so this was before I had gotten married. One night I dreamed I was talking to her. I wanted to hug her and she said, "Baby [as she often called me, being the youngest in my family], you know you can't do that, but be sure to get the brakes fixed on the car." Then I woke up. I told my father about my dream, and we pondered its meaning. We had the brakes checked on our vehicles and found no problems. However, after my mother died, my father gave my mother's car to one of my sisters, Odessa, who lived in another state. We called and told her to get the brakes checked out. She called us back a few days later and told us the mechanic was surprised the brakes hadn't already failed. He wanted to know how we knew to bring the vehicle in. We didn't— the Lord did.

People have asked how and why do I hear answers to my prayers when so few people do. I don't know. Perhaps it's an indication of how hardheaded I am. I can't help but notice that when I do hear a voice, I almost always have to be told something twice. I'm trying to be a better listener and a better follower of the promptings of the Spirit.

I take to heart the scripture in Doctrine and Covenants 90:24, which says, "Search diligently, pray always, and be believing, and all things shall work together for your good."

I take that scripture literally, that all will work together not only for my good but for the good of the Lord's work and His glory.

President Gordon B. Hinckley, writes in *Stand a Little Taller,* "Adulation is poison. It is so very important that you do not let praise and adulation go to your head. Never lose sight of the fact that the Lord put you where you are according to His design, which you don't fully understand.

Acknowledge the Lord for whatever good you can accomplish and give Him the credit and the glory" (p. 5). I tell of these experiences not to boast of myself but to boast of the orchestration of the Lord's hand in all things. Before and during my mission I did not fully understand His design in having me complete my four generations before going on a mission. While on my mission, I did not fully understand His design in having me paired with elderly sister companions. I have learned the importance of doing what the Lord asks when He asks me to do it instead of waiting a couple of days until I remember or get around to it.

Prayer is our daily, vital link to Heavenly Father. As Bishop H. Burke Peterson says in "Adversity and Prayer," in *Prayer* (pp. 108–9): "As you feel the need to confide in the Lord or to improve the quality of your visits with him—to pray, if you please—may I suggest a process to follow: go where you can be alone, where you can think, where you can kneel, where you can speak out loud to him. The bedroom, the bathroom, or a closet will do. Now, picture him in your mind's eye. Think to whom you are speaking. Control your thoughts—don't let them wander. Address him as your Father and your friend. Now tell him things you really feel to tell him—not trite phrases that have little meaning, but a sincere, heartfelt conversation with him. Confide in Him. Ask him for forgiveness. Plead with him. Enjoy him. Thank him. Express your love to him. Then listen for his answers.

"Listening is an essential part of praying. Answers from the Lord come quietly, ever so quietly. In fact, few hear his answers audibly with their ears. We must be listening carefully or we will never recognize them. Most answers from the Lord are felt in our hearts as a warm, comfortable expression, or they may come as thoughts to our minds. They come to those who are prepared and who are patient. . . . For [your] own good [you] must take the first step, and this step is prayer."

ABOUT THE AUTHOR

Derek Dowsett DBD Productions 2004

Jerri A. Harwell was born and raised in Detroit, Michigan. She has her own business, EDIT-WELL, and is a freelance writer and editor. This is her first full length book. She is also adjunct faculty/instructor at Salt Lake Community College where she teaches developmental writing. In addition, Jerri does a one woman portrayal of Jane Elizabeth Manning James, an early Black Mormon pioneer at This Is the Place Heritage State Park in Salt Lake City, Utah. Jerri also wrote the script for her portrayal.

She and her husband, Donald L. Harwell, have been married seventeen years and reside in Salt Lake City, Utah. They have six children, four of whom are still at home. Don serves as President of The Genesis Group, which is the LDS Church's official auxiliary for Black Latter-day Saints, organized in 1971. In addition, he serves on his Stake High Council for the Midvale Utah Union Fort Stake.

Jerri was the Senior Editor for The Genesis Group's newsletter, which serves as a communication tool for African-American members of the Church around the world. She has served in two Relief Society Presidencies; taught in Relief Society, Sunday School, and Primary; and held numerous other callings in the LDS Church.

She often accepts speaking assignments for firesides, sacrament meetings, symposiums, conferences, and conventions. In 2004, she was a presenter at BYU's Women's Conference speaking about prayer.